101 Unnecessary Inventions
Copyright © 2019 Matty Benedetto

All rights reserved. This book or any portion thereof may not be reproduced or used in any manner whatsoever without the express written permission of the publisher except for the use of brief quotations in a book review.

First Edition, 2019

Burlington, VT

Unnecessary Inventions
www.unnecessaryinventions.com

101 Unnecessary Inventions

Products that solve problems that don't exist

Matty Benedetto

Welcome to Unnecessary Inventions! All of the products you are about to encounter have been created by the evil genius Matty Benedetto.

As a self-taught product designer, Matty loves to experiment with unconventional design practices to create his inventions that are truly unnecessary for anyone to use in their daily life.

Each new invention is created within his studio in Burlington, Vermont using unique production methods from 3D printing, mold making, sewing, woodworking, baking, and whatever else he can get his hands on.

These inventions have been seen far and wide across the depths of the internet and onto the pages of the book you now hold in your hand.

Under no circumstances should you ever try to convince yourself any of these inventions are actually necessary as they solve issues that simply do not actually exist.

Enjoy.

Lego Socks™ Can anyone tell me why stepping on a Lego is the worst pain in the world? Well time to say adios to that excruciating experience when you slip on these comfortable socks. Each pair features a flexible sole with a geometric hole pattern to simply pick up each brick without harm. No clean up your toys or you aren't getting any dessert!!

Marathon Utility Controller™ It's about to be an all weekend gaming marathon and I'm not leaving the couch! Our new 9-in-1 ultimate utility game controller has everything you need for extended gaming including a smartphone lockbox, a deodorant stick, a handy extra finger, an electric fan, a chin rest, cup holder, removable toothbrush, beef jerky dispenser, and a rear view mirror.

StubStoppers™ It can be like a construction zone trying to get around your apartment barefoot without stubbing your toes on something. Equip your big toe with these pint sized hard hats to say goodbye to bruised toes and show that furniture leg who's boss!

The 12oz Shirt™ It's 5 O'clock somewhere! Dress up for work and ready for happy hour all at the same time with our exciting new button down work shirt with built in cup holder. Pop a brew and bring it with you.

JiffyCuts™ Trim your nails in one single CRUNCH! If you have been wasting hours on hours clipping each individual nail, you have been living in the past. Welcome to the future with our all in one nail cutting solution. Slide in each nail and with one squeeze down to cut them down to size!

The SockLocker™ Sick and tired of always losing just one of your favorite socks?! Completely turn your life around with our handy little sock storage device so you never misplace any of your precious socks. Three proprietary sock hangers are included to neatly and safely hang your sock collection. Now where the hell did I put my foot cream??

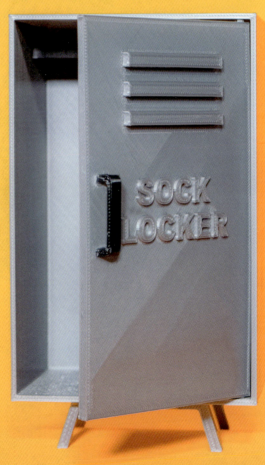

The Unnecessary Membership Card™ Forged from the center of the earth, this matte black metal card features a mesmerizing pattern and Ui logo cut from diamonds, a photon-laser cut membership insignia, and a hand painted scripture on the back. The Unnecessary Membership Card entitles you to: Absolutely NO Perks, ZERO Membership Benefits, and Unnecessary Space Taken From Your Wallet.

OneCan TrashCan™ Every rogue soda can, fallen solider beer, and all those LaCroix cans laying around the office have officially met their match. Pick up a six pack of these perfectly sized trash cans to always have a place to put your empties. Don't forget the 100 Can Party Pack for your next rager!

RealityCheck5000™ While you are on the grind to up your Instagram follower count, the world population that is not following you is growing at an exponential rate. Our futuristic algorithm takes into account the changing birth and death rates around the world and subtracts your current Instagram follow count. Is it your daily motivation or disparity, you decide.

Pizza FannyPack™ Precious pizza, anywhere - anytime! Strap on our futuristic fanny pack that features two transparent pouches for your favorite slices on the go! The rugged waist strap has a high impact resistant buckle and reflector for a safe Pizza Party on the go. Extra pineapple please!

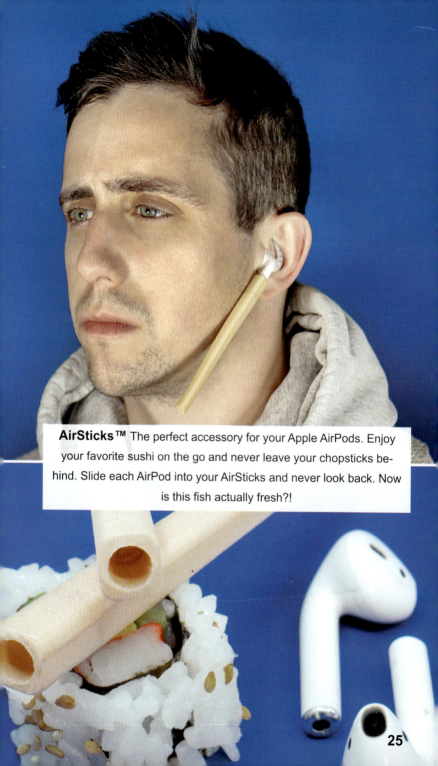

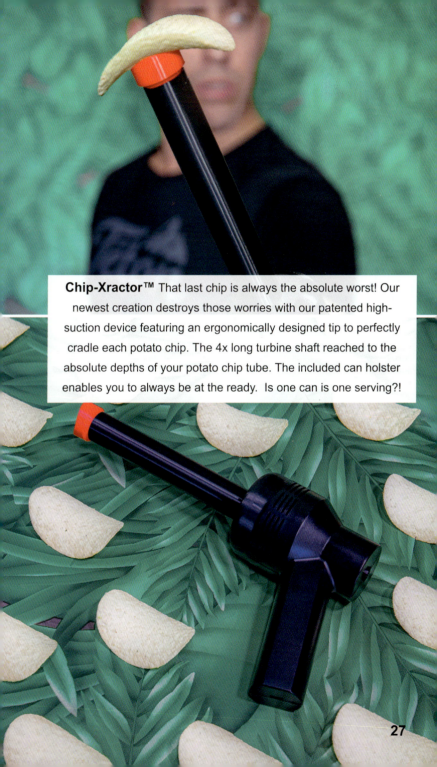

Chip-Xractor™ That last chip is always the absolute worst! Our newest creation destroys those worries with our patented high-suction device featuring an ergonomically designed tip to perfectly cradle each potato chip. The 4x long turbine shaft reached to the absolute depths of your potato chip tube. The included can holster enables you to always be at the ready. Is one can is one serving?!

PuppyThumbs™ If dogs are a man's best friend, don't you think they deserve opposable thumbs?! A breakthrough in our technology now allows any dog to control these realistically designed, canine specific thumbs through an advanced neural network built on an AI engine. Regardless of how they work, your dog will never play fetch the same way again. Where my dawgs at?!

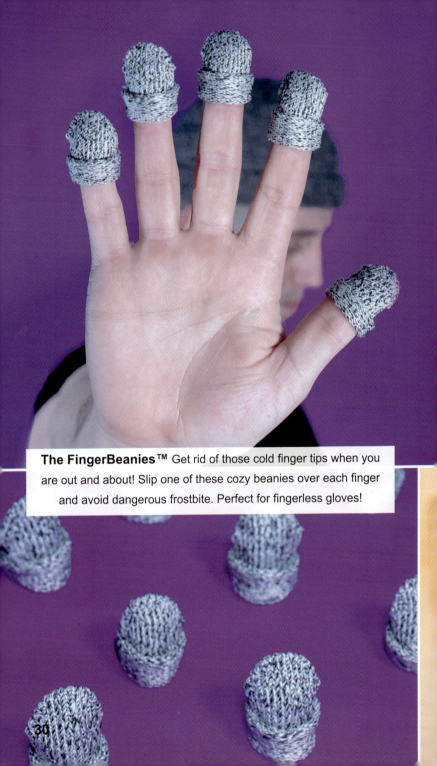

The FingerBeanies™ Get rid of those cold finger tips when you are out and about! Slip one of these cozy beanies over each finger and avoid dangerous frostbite. Perfect for fingerless gloves!

Taco Fraiche™ Exfoliate with the zest of Cinco de Mayo year round with with exhilarating spray mist. With hint of authentic seasoning, cilantro, red onions, and tomatoes, you can turn any food into a taco delight or exfoliate your senses with a light facial mist awakening.

RoadHold™ Every single car needs more cup holders. Stop wasting perfect real estate around your steering wheel and have your favorite drinks at hand when you are out and about. Choose the perfect spot around the steering wheel of your car and snap on this perfect cup holder. For best results, use when driving on straight roads & highways. Who's ready for a road trip!

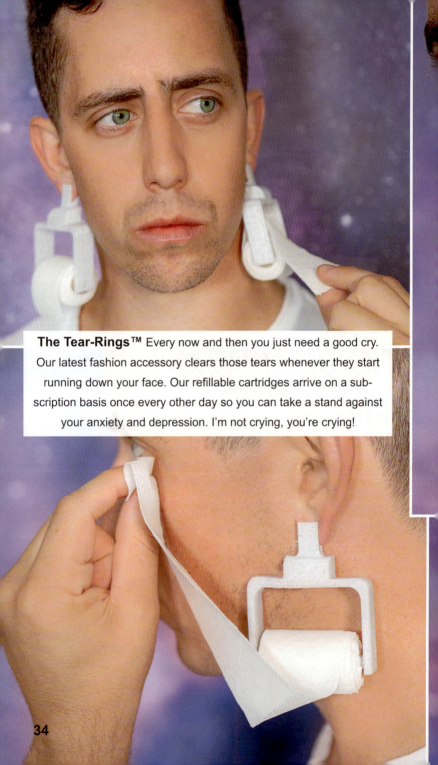

The Tear-Rings™ Every now and then you just need a good cry. Our latest fashion accessory clears those tears whenever they start running down your face. Our refillable cartridges arrive on a subscription basis once every other day so you can take a stand against your anxiety and depression. I'm not crying, you're crying!

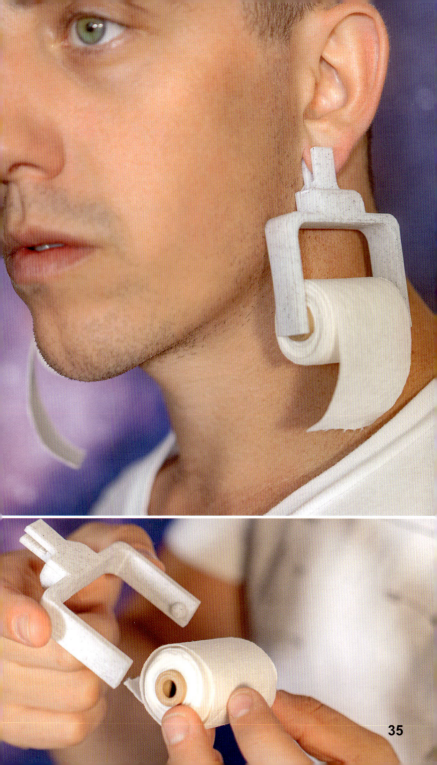

The PlanterPisser™ When you gotta go, you just gotta go! Now have the ease of taking a quick bathroom break any time nature calls. Quickly stab this portable urinal into any plant pot, garden bed, or even a vase to get the relief you need. Don't forget to zip your fly!

The Baguette Pack™ I know, I know...FINALLY a backpack specially designed for your delicious baguette. Hit your local bakery and pick up some steaming hot freshly baked bread knowing you will keep it safe, protected, and dry all the way home. Slide this French delicacy into our ergonomically designed pouch and cinch it up to be on your way in no time!

The Wake Up Box™ Strobe yourself awake to get your day going before you know it. This high powered box features four insanely bright LED panels to blast multiple patented light patterns in your face to scientifically wake yourself up faster than ever before. Simply grab the two stainless steel handles and insert your head into the box.

Cosmic Catcher 2000™ Who is ready to storm Area51?! Be prepared when you come across a slimey Martian with our high powered cosmic net gun. Bring your bike pump to build up the pressure within the cannon and send the net flying across the air! Those aliens never stood a chance!

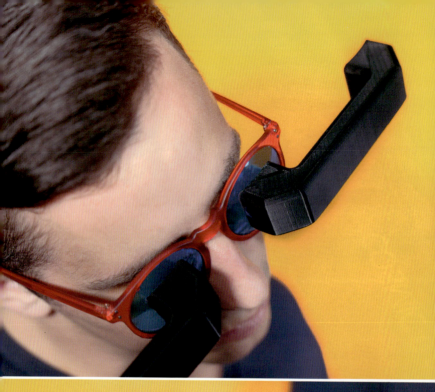

LookBak Spectacles™ You need to be careful these days - you never know who might be lurking behind you. Luckily we are proud to introduce our new triple prism sunglasses which allow you to always keep a close watch of what's going on around your back. Never miss a thing when you hit the streets with these bad boys on. Tell those haters, Deal with It!

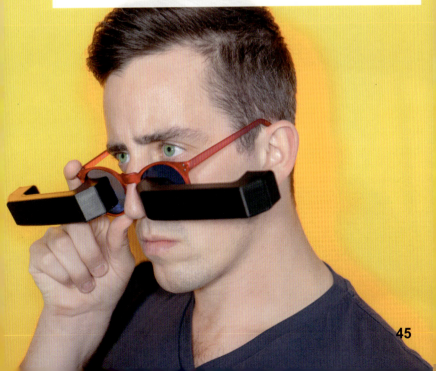

Gator Grips™ Your dad's favorite rubbery holed shoes are now available for your hands. As the first ever pair of Gloves of it's kind they feature all the best things from the shoes you love, including that thick foam material and safety strap. Start getting all your household chores done in style.

The Cease & Desist™ A certain company wasn't too excited about the original name of the Gator Grips. So let's just call them the Unnecessary Invention formally known as the (Company which shall not be named) Gloves...Oops!

CookieMitts™ Take a bite outta this! The all day wearable snack has arrived in the form of gooey sugary mittens. If you are enjoying this delicious outfit accessory solo or offering someone your thumb, enjoy three layers of chocolate chip delight. Find your favorite frosting and dip away right into your mouth.

RotarySMS™ Text your besties like it's 1969! Our new smartphone attachment brings back the good old days of rotary phones but with a new 2019 twist. Plug the device into your smartphone and start spinning away letter by letter to send your next message. Whether you simply miss the classic rotary phone days or just want to be a hipster, we got you covered.

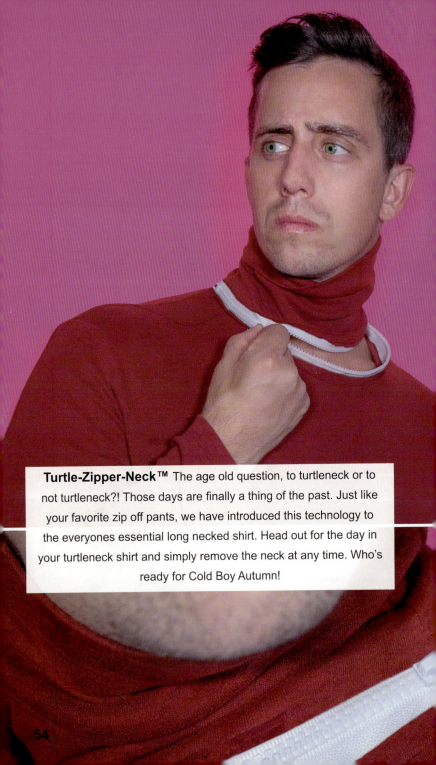

Turtle-Zipper-Neck™ The age old question, to turtleneck or to not turtleneck?! Those days are finally a thing of the past. Just like your favorite zip off pants, we have introduced this technology to the everyones essential long necked shirt. Head out for the day in your turtleneck shirt and simply remove the neck at any time. Who's ready for Cold Boy Autumn!

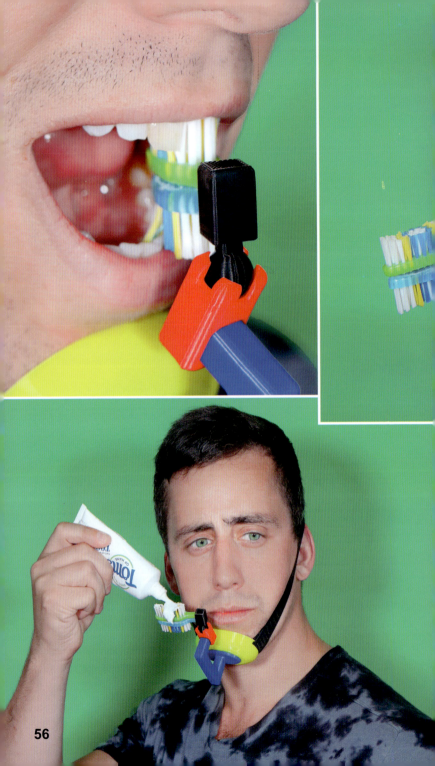

Freehand Toothbrush™ Let's be real, who has time for dental hygiene?! Well now you can go about your day and get your teeth squeaky clean completely hands free. Strap our newest innovation over your head to enjoy a dual sided toothbrush that easily swivels around your mouth. Grind your teeth against the bristles and shine on. Say cheese!

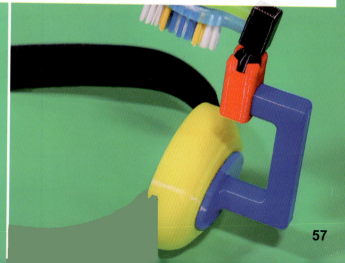

NeverSpiller™ Hold my beer, it's gunna be a bumpy ride! Strap on the beer stein attachment for your electronic gimbal and hit the club. Never spill a single drop of your precious micro-brew when you are dancing, shuffle through a crowd, or simply getting adventurous. It's 5 o'clock somewhere, CHEERS!

Unfold-o-matic™ It's time to get ready to head out but everything you want to wear is neatly folded up in your closet. Well now you can perfectly unfold your favorite shirts in a snap! Simply place the shirt face up and use each of our four smooth bending arms to hook and unfold! It really couldn't be more simple than this to get dressed.

CaseSquared™ Yup, it's a Case for your Smartphone Case. Stop scuffing up that spiffy new case but still show it off with pride in our transparent silicone buffer case. It conveniently slides over your current case to keep it minty fresh like the day you bought. The bubble wrap style bumpers make it the ultimate fashion meets function accessory.

The Damn That Bathroom Handle Is Gross I Ain't Touching It™ Are you hands glistening from being freshly cleansed but that bathroom handle is disgusting on another level. Never leave the house again without the extra handle grip extension. A germaphobes delight!

The Digits Comb™ It's time for you to always have that natural good hair day look! Whenever you just don't want to run your hands through your hair, simply use our silicone fingers comb. Breeze through your hair as if you would be doing it with your own hands to get each stand back in it place. Time for a selfie!!

The FrustrationBuckle™ Slow walkers?! Confused Tourists?! Ugh they can just make my blood boil! Luckily this handy new belt buckle will let out that frustration and get those people OUT. OF. YOUR. WAY. Just continually push the center of the buckle to unleash the fury!

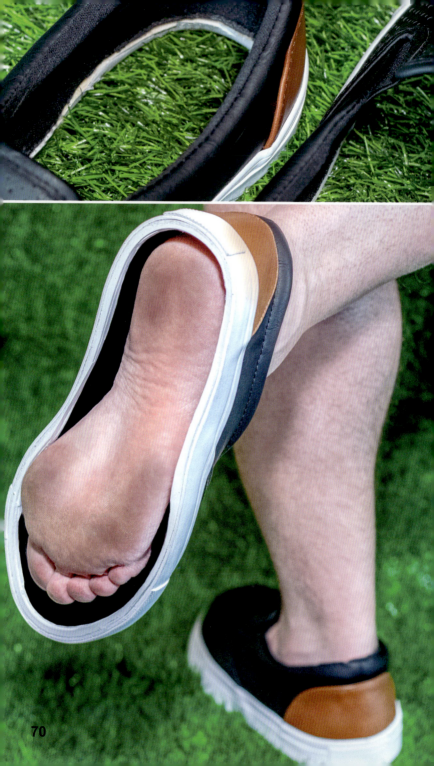

Incognito Kicks™ Ah! Feel the ground beneath you where ever you go. Slip on these comfortable loafers and enjoy the sensation of walking barefoot while maintaining the appearance of appropriate attire. No soles, no problem! Incognito mode ACTIVATED!

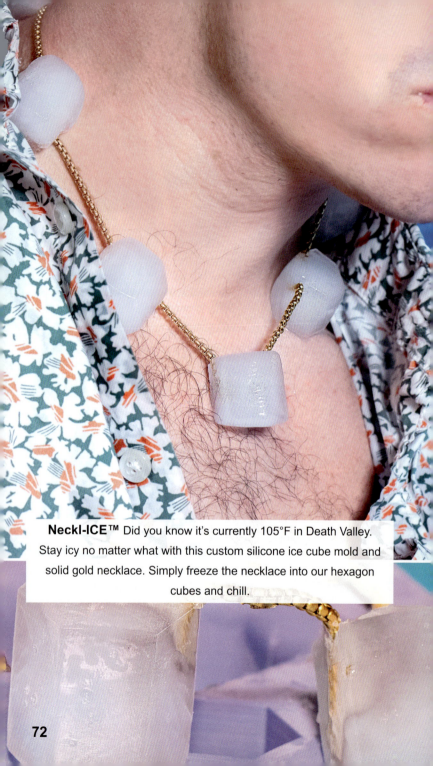

SuperSolar Shirt™ When the sun is out that now means a fully charged phone. Strut your stuff out and about with our newest solar panel shirt with dual USB charging ports. Lay in the hot sun all day to get your smartphone back to 100% with absolute ease. Renewable energy meets high fashion - don't forget the sunscreen!

Sip n Curl™ When it's 5 O'Clock hit the gym and enjoy a nice cold beer all at the same time. One thousand one, one thousand two, one thousand three, one thousand four...

RightRound Cone™ Eating your Ice Cream cone just got kicked into high gear. Introducing our drill bit ice cream cone extension kit! Strap on our universal bit, slide in your favorite ice cream, and full throttle ahead. Ahhhh brain freeze

Gummy Human Centipedes™ Happy Halloween, It's the spookiest month of the year! To get ready for the big day, we created the most delicately gummies to give out to Trick-or-Treaters this year! Chomp on this miniature Human Centipedes (which happens to be our favorite movie) and feel the sugary rush!

UtilityNails™ The newest tool box must have just arrived! For any home improvement job simply secure these rugged steel nails with superglue and have all your tools at the tips of your hands. It features wrenches, screwdrivers, and an Allen key! It Tool Time!

THIS PAGE WAS UNNECESSARILY LEFT BLANK

I'M HONESTLY NOT SURE IF THIS ONE WAS OR WASN'T

Rake 'n Prance™ Cleaning your lawn this Autumn is now a walk in the park. Grab this strap-on rake for your favorite shoes and get to work. Quickly strut around and clean up all the fallen leaves while your jealous neighbors watch in awe.
The moonwalk has never been more productive

Snackmingo™ This is what heaven looks like - pool snacks floating all around you at all times. Meet the newest innovation in snack technology. Always have your snacks in sight with our inflatable neon flamingo and our triple locked airtight bag that hangs underwater to keep your snacks in reach for your pruned fingers to chow down. CANNONBALL!

The Kazuul™ Do you have music running through your veins but need some nicotine in there too? Introducing our revolutionary Vape & Kazoo combo device. Belt out your favorite tune while taking a hit your vape.

2Spouts1Bottle™ This is the absolute easiest way to share your favorite tasty beverage with your BFF. Our dual sided squirt bottle fills up from either end and can fit an entire 2 Liters. Get ready for a battle royale for the last drop!

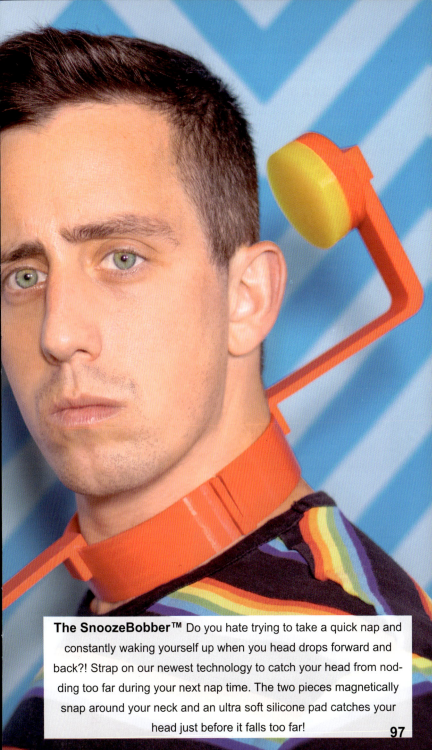

Avocado On A Stick™ Every millennial loves avocado toast! Now make your favorite snack faster than ever at home or on the go...on a stick! Roll up and sub on your favorite slice of krispy toast!

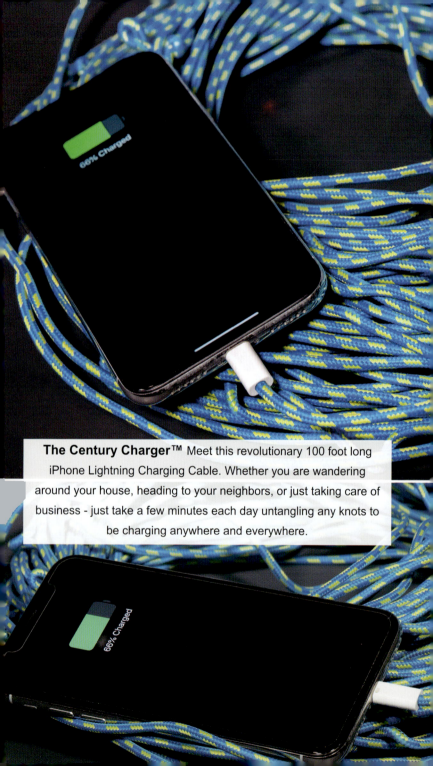

The Century Charger™ Meet this revolutionary 100 foot long iPhone Lightning Charging Cable. Whether you are wandering around your house, heading to your neighbors, or just taking care of business - just take a few minutes each day untangling any knots to be charging anywhere and everywhere.

FingerTrack™ These days your fingers need to make it through a full day texting on your smartphone so it's more important than ever to get a true full body work out. Build muscle and burn calories in your fingers so they are ready to go any time!

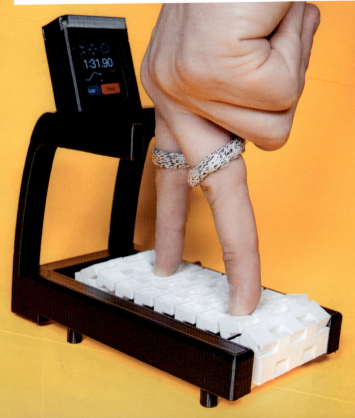

CargoMAX™ Everyone knows that you can NEVER have enough cargo pockets on your pants. Mix and match all your favorite cargo pockets with my patent pending modular pocket pants. Different colors, styles, and sizes so you have somewhere to put all your essentials. High Fashion too!

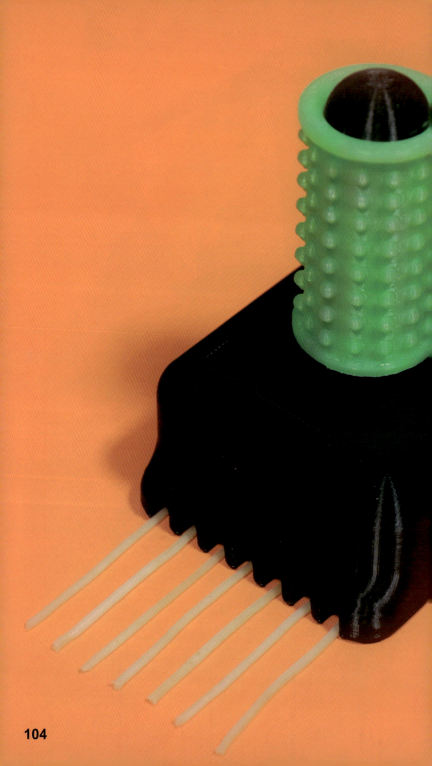

The Sketti Straightener™ Why is spaghetti just one of the most unorganized meals you can possibly eat?! It's time to get your noodles in order and start eating dinner like a civilized human being. Go from a humbles mess to perfectly organized pasta parade. Now who brought the meatballs!

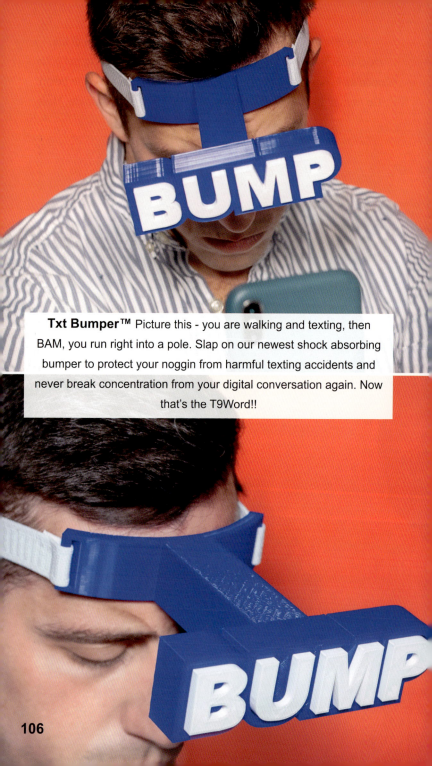

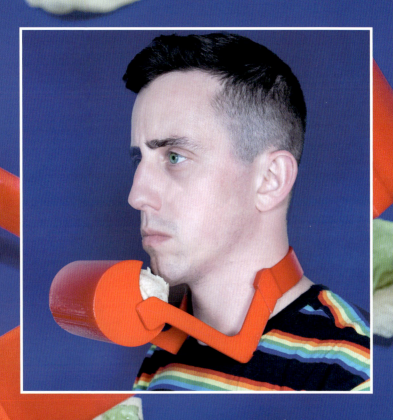

The BurritoTrough™ Enjoy a delicious burrito hands free! Whether you are on the go or having a lazy day, quickly and easily fill up on your favorite Mexican meal. Strap this easy device around your neck and attack it sideways.

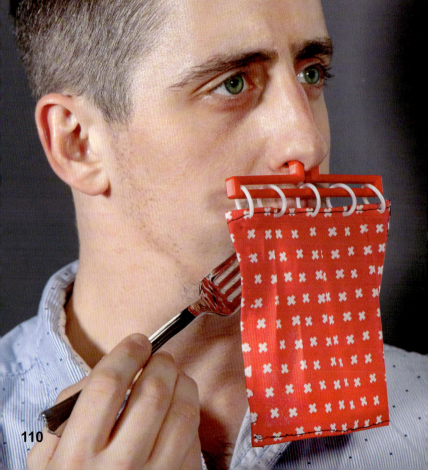

Cuisine Curtain™ Enjoy your 5 star meal in complete privacy. Attach this personal curtain to your nose to cover your mouth during any meal and never worry about chewing with your mouth open. Quickly slide it open during conversation or a phone call with ease.

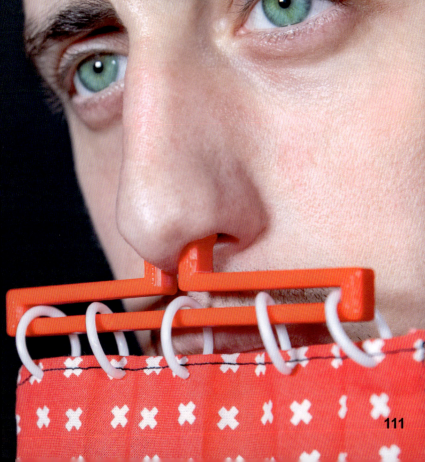

Luke Warm Coffee™ Finally enjoy coffee the way it was intended to be served, at room temperature. Our new signature roast has been perfected to be enjoyed at a balmy 72°. Ditch the hot and cold brews, and simply keep our blend un-refrigerated in your home to enjoy our 100% GMO coffee anytime.

HandyBowl™ Who's hungry?! Whether you are late for work or just munching on the go, strap on our portable cereal bowl for breakfast whenever. Just hold your arm up and flat to enjoy your favorite sugar filled cereal.

Glovetensils™ It's dinner time right from the tips of your fingers. Stop fumbling around with oversized utensils to enjoy your favorite meal and slide these on! Each finger of these knit gloves feature a specific piece from your cutlery set from a fork, knife, spoon, spatula, and skewer. Now eat your peas or your not getting dessert!

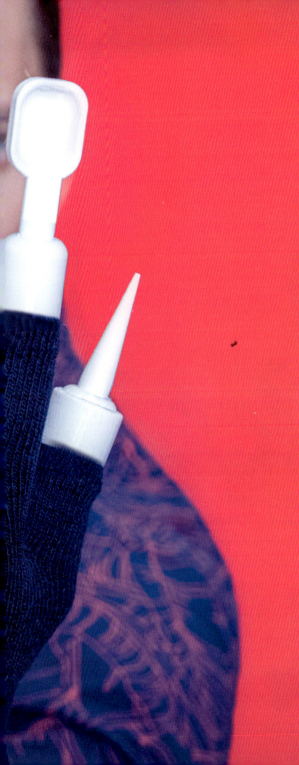

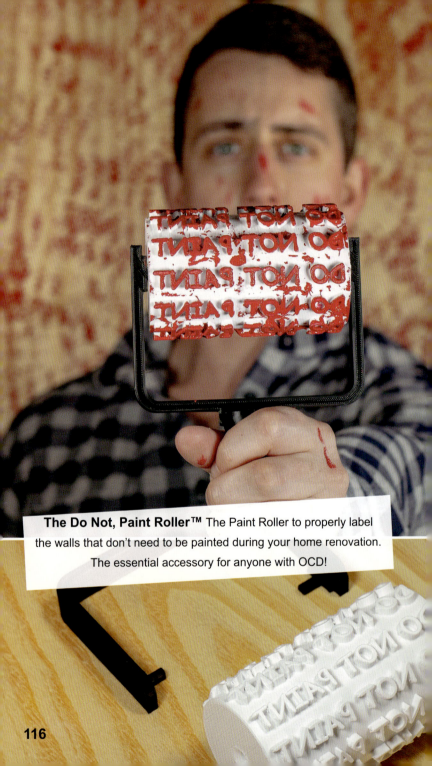

The Do Not, Paint Roller™ The Paint Roller to properly label the walls that don't need to be painted during your home renovation. The essential accessory for anyone with OCD!

The Hoverbrella™ Enjoy a rainy day without the hassle of having to carry an umbrella. Go hands free and a stay completely dry as it follows you around wherever you need to go!

The FurRoller™ Start telling all your friends that you got a dog and cover all your clothes in fur. Choose your favorite breed of dog and roll your heart out.

Heels Wheels™ Learn to strut like a professional. Get used to walking in those stilettos with these training wheels for heels. Simply slide them onto your favorite pair and safety practice your walk with confidence. Sashay away!

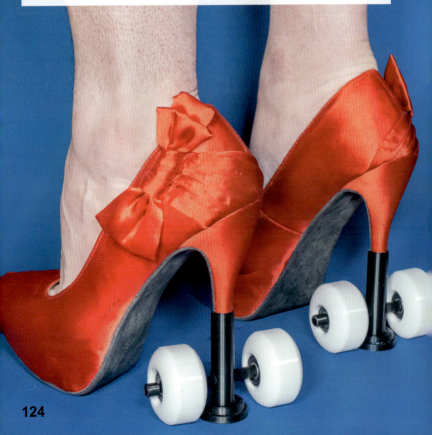

Hide-A-Jack™ You no longer need to be embarrassed when using your older model smartphone that clearly still has a headphone jack. This handy keychain slides directly in to discretely hide it when you just want to just feel like everyone else with an iPhone X. If you just can't take the criticism after a long day, flip it over and crack open a beer.

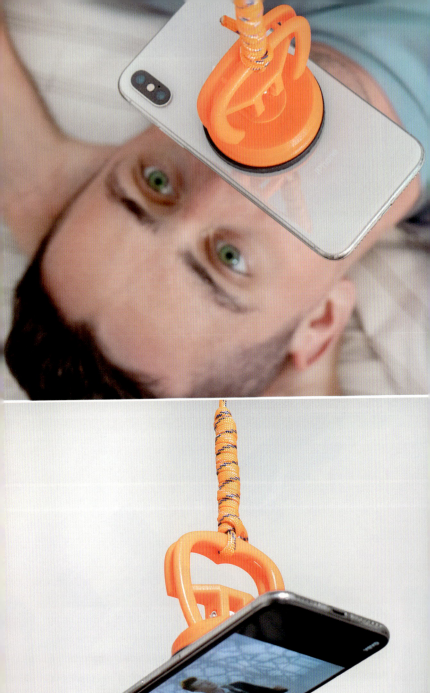

iDangle™ Stop dropping your phone on that precious face of yours in bed! Suspend and dangle your phone hands-free just inches from your face to binge that new season on Netflix. The NASA grade suction cup grips the back of your phone - while the Army ballistic paracord hangs all the way down from the ceiling.

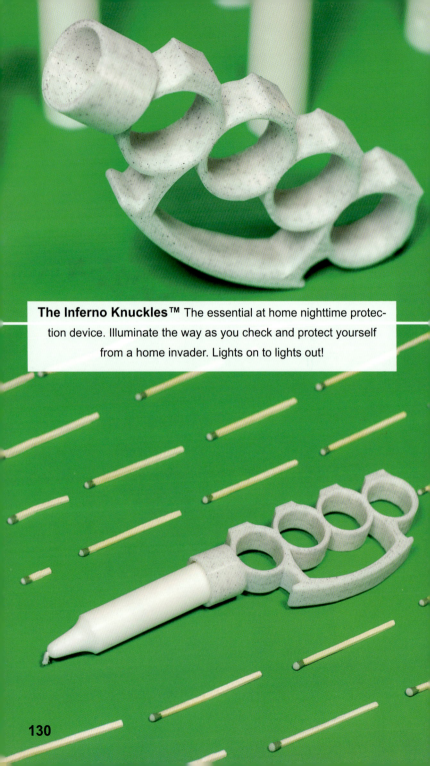

The Inferno Knuckles™ The essential at home nighttime protection device. Illuminate the way as you check and protect yourself from a home invader. Lights on to lights out!

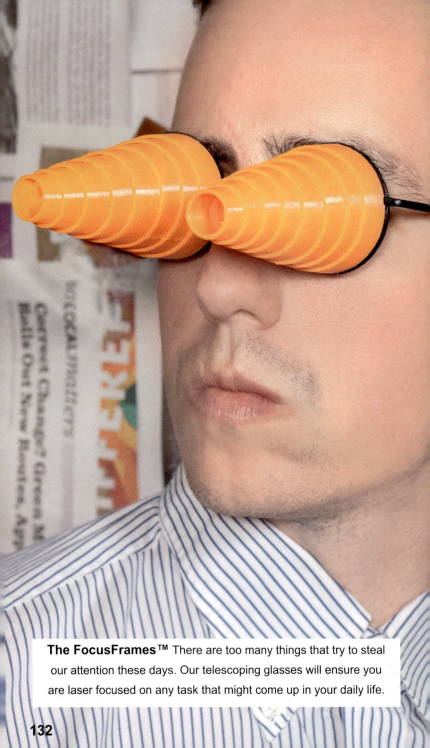

The FocusFrames™ There are too many things that try to steal our attention these days. Our telescoping glasses will ensure you are laser focused on any task that might come up in your daily life.

The Infinity Saucelet™ In one snap of my fingers all your fast food dreams will come to life. This extremely powerful gauntlet can wield the power of all of your favorite fast food sauces all at once. Cover everything in sauce... whatever it takes.

InstaParasol™ Somehow just one little drop of rain puts your touchscreen into crisis mode. Swipe, double tap, and type with confidence in the rain with the perfect umbrella ergonomically designed so snap onto any smartphone. Always put your phone's priority ahead of your own.

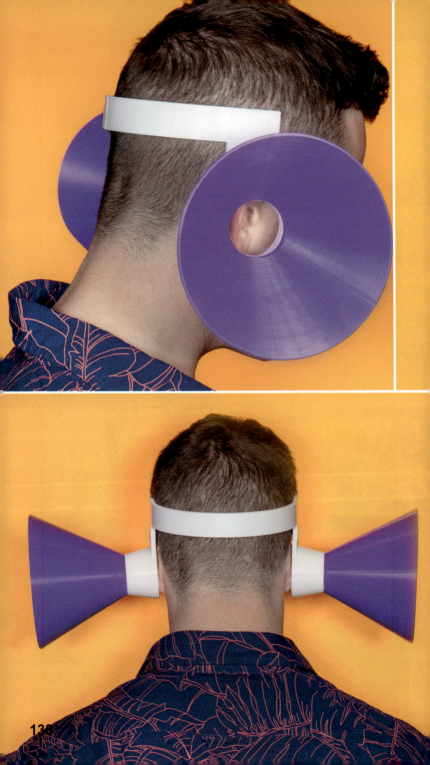

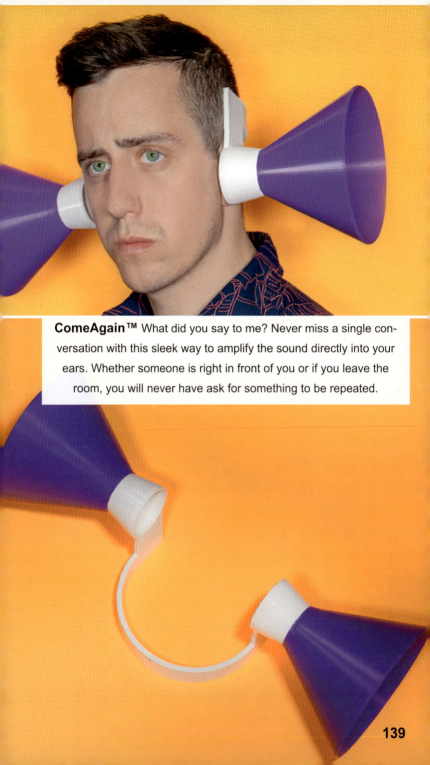

ComeAgain™ What did you say to me? Never miss a single conversation with this sleek way to amplify the sound directly into your ears. Whether someone is right in front of you or if you leave the room, you will never have ask for something to be repeated.

My Perfect Hogan™ Have you always been jealous of Hulk Hogan's pristine handle bar mustache? Look no further with this new shaving staple to get the perfect replica handle bar mustache for your face.

The No Booze Ice Cube Tray™ Trying to drink less during the week but still craving your favorite cocktail? Ditch the booze while still mixing yourself a "Vodka" cocktail with this no calorie alternative. Drink Unnecessarily...I mean Responsibly.

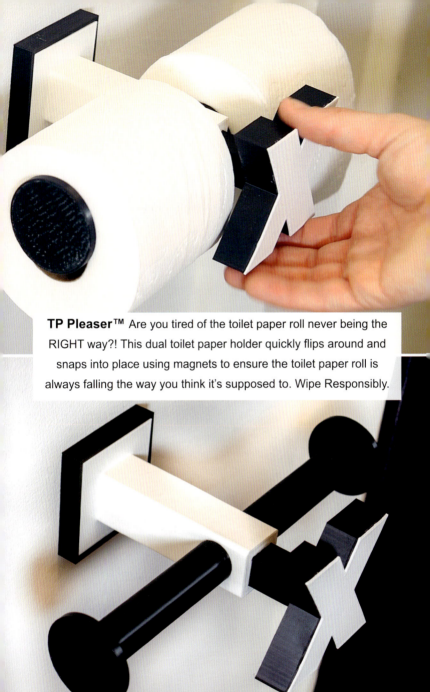

TP Pleaser™ Are you tired of the toilet paper roll never being the RIGHT way?! This dual toilet paper holder quickly flips around and snaps into place using magnets to ensure the toilet paper roll is always falling the way you think it's supposed to. Wipe Responsibly.

SunShaders™ Get more of your sunglasses with your own shades for your shades. Whether you need to block out more light, spy through the blinds, or block out haters - wear them up, down, or closed with your favorite pair of sunglasses.

The PersonalSpacinator™ We all have had those times with close talkers, random people in public, and simply wanting to be left alone. Reclaim the personal space around you so no one can get within your special area for whatever reason. Available in 3ft, 5ft and 10ft spacers. Now GTFO!

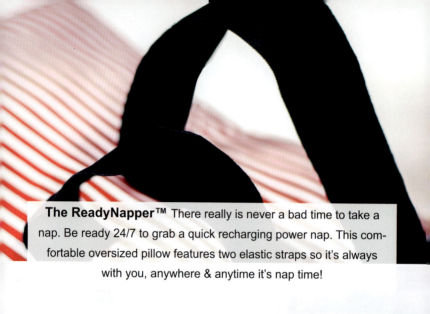

The ReadyNapper™ There really is never a bad time to take a nap. Be ready 24/7 to grab a quick recharging power nap. This comfortable oversized pillow features two elastic straps so it's always with you, anywhere & anytime it's nap time!

Slice Slicer™ Everyone gets their own perfect pizza slice! Divide your favorite pizza pie into perfectly even slices with just a few chops with this eight blade slicer. More pepperoni please!

Bang Brows™ The hottest beauty trend of the season has arrived! It's time for your eyebrows to take center stage and steal the show. These eyebrow extensions give your eyes the bangs they have always been hoping for. Simply add these brow attachment to spice up any look from casual to elegant. There's a new beauty influencer on the block...

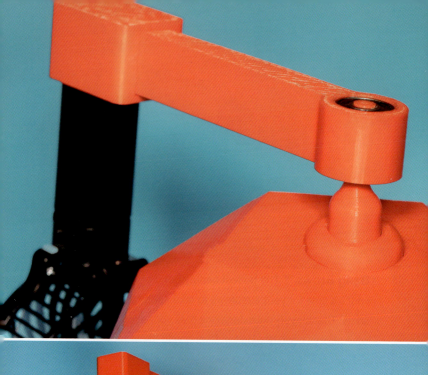
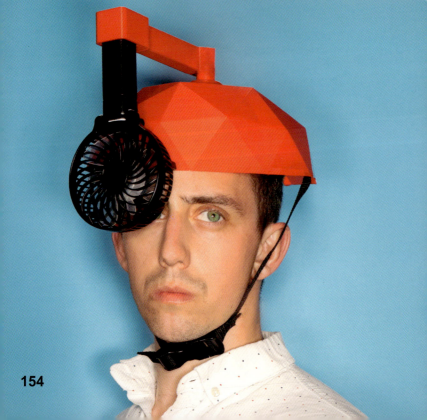

The Smellmet™ Did Karen bring fish for lunch again or maybe Chad has too much cologne on? This odor blocking helmet conveniently spins a high powered fan around your head to dispel any foul smells. Surround yourself with only the air!

SweatGutters™ The summer heat is upon us and I am already not sure I can take the sweating. Luckily now you can easily collect and remove of any sweat before it hits your face. Easily dispel any perspiration from your forehead and away from your body.

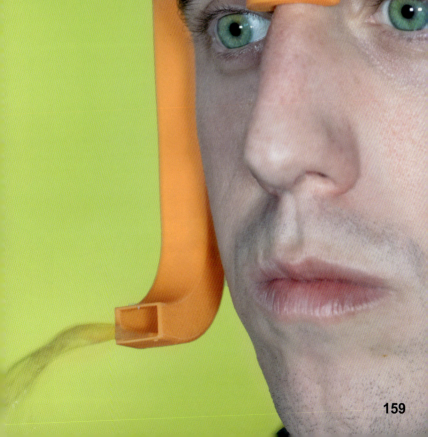

The FlopFlips™ Reverse your steps to ditch that stalker on the beach. These sandals feature a backwards sole to ensure all your footprints always appear to be traveling the opposite direction you are walking. About Face!

Straw2Go™ Let's get rid of plastic straws and save the world! When you are on the go, don't forget this rugged plastic carrying case for your favorite metal straw! It quickly snaps together with magnets and with your help we rid this world of those evil plastic tubes.

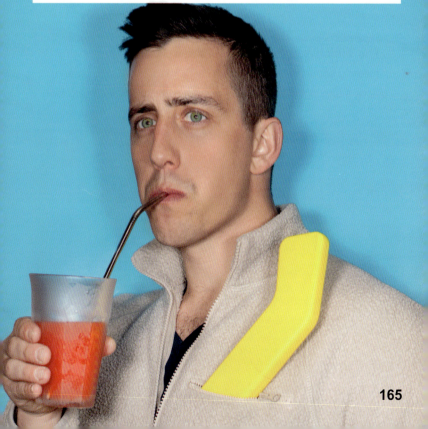

The WhichWay™ Say goodbye to the directional dance when meeting someone in your path. This harness easily slips on and places a turn signal on each of your shoulders to let on coming foot traffic which way you're headed.

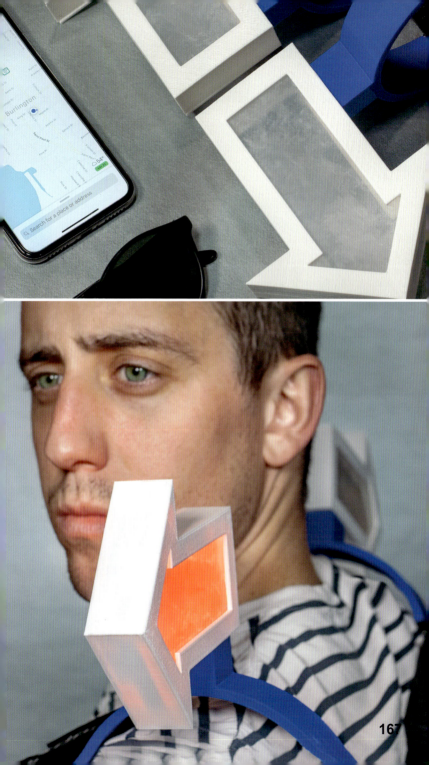

The Finglonger™ Reach new heights like never before! Extend your abilities on any finger to finally reach what you simply never could before.

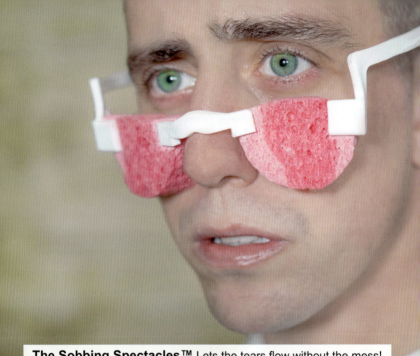

The Sobbing Spectacles™ Lets the tears flow without the mess! Our newly released glasses feature two highly absorbent sponges to soak up all those salty tears before they run down your face and simply ring them out before your next use. Whether it's a sad movie, a wedding, or just your nightly cry before bed - never shed a tear without these beauties.

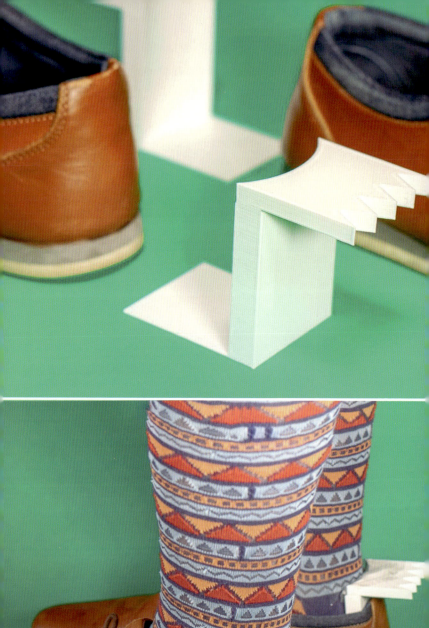

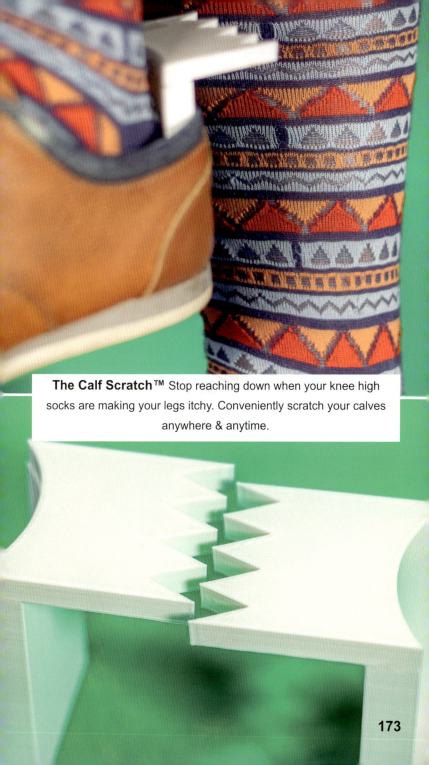

The Calf Scratch™ Stop reaching down when your knee high socks are making your legs itchy. Conveniently scratch your calves anywhere & anytime.

The ForkYou™ Never have your condiments touch or mix with this click activated condiment fork. Carefully fill each compartment and chow down.

The LookBak™ Never miss a thing with your own personal rear view mirror anywhere you go! The elastic band stretch around your arm while the mirror sits perfectly in view on your shoulder.

StickyKicks™ Stand your ground whether you are stuck in a hurricane, holding your place in a crowd, or just not doing anywhere anytime soon! These suction cup platforms attach to any of your your favorite shoes. Kick those sticky situations goodbye!

iWipe Pro Max™ Apple isn't the only ones who are capable of innovation. With the brand new triple lens system of the iPhone 11 Pro, we wanted to ensure your lenses always are crystal clean for every phone. Strap on this revolutionary accessory to your iPhone and let it wipe away all of your grit & grime. Now smile for the camera!

The Hÿpēr Båg™ When putting together your next IKEA furniture piece, take a few deep breaths and don't stress when you can't figure out the directions. Make sure you don't hyperventilate!

The Front2Back Case™ Quit only getting photos of your friends when you know you are looking good! The Front2Back Case combines two iPhone cases that perfect expose the cameras in each direction, so you can always have your second spare iPhone with you. Selfie away.

The Plug of Thrones™ Are you avoiding spoilers from tonights episode of Game of Thrones or simply tired of hearing everyone talk about it?! Conveniently have a pair of earplug anytime you don't want to hear about the new season 8 premiere, whatever your reason is.

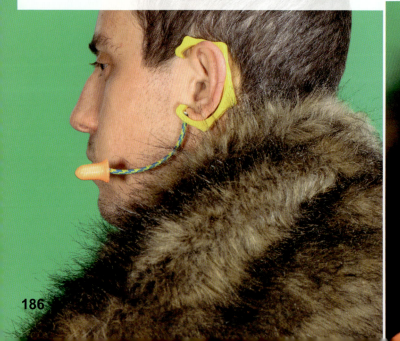

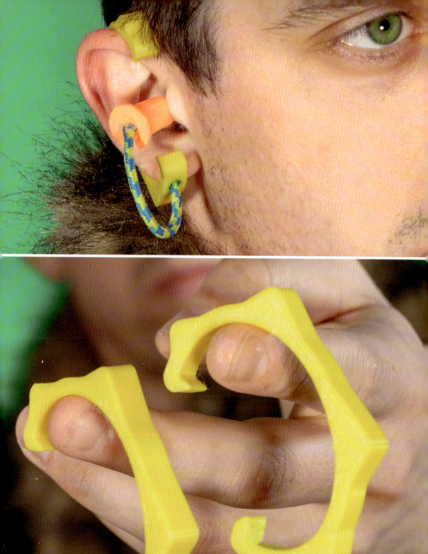

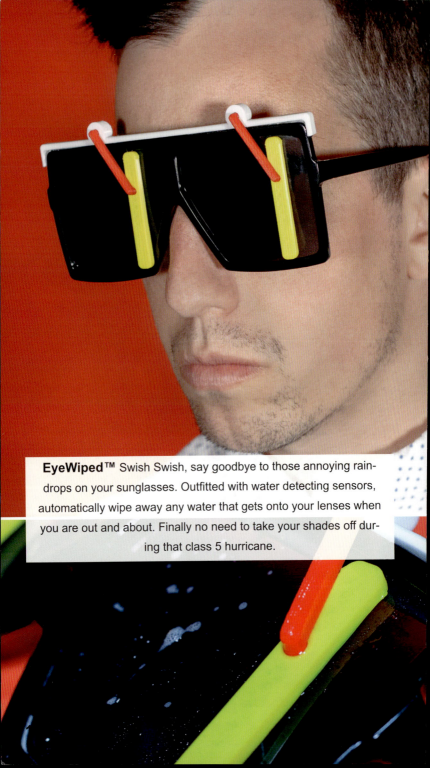

EyeWiped™ Swish Swish, say goodbye to those annoying raindrops on your sunglasses. Outfitted with water detecting sensors, automatically wipe away any water that gets onto your lenses when you are out and about. Finally no need to take your shades off during that class 5 hurricane.

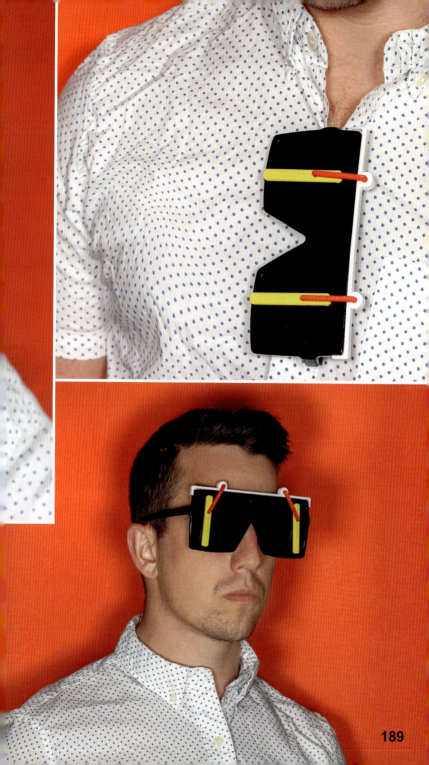

The PillowOne S ™ Meet the bed in a box for your smartphone to compliment your new age mattress. Your phone works just as hard as you do, it deserves a good night charge.

The Anywhere Hook ™ Your personal coat hook that goes with you anywhere that you go. Simply attach it within the collar of your favorite shirt and sling your coat behind you throughout the entire day! Now did anyone check if it was even supposed to rain today?

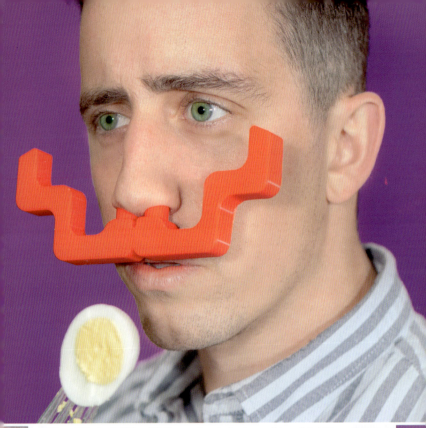

The Stink-A-Way™ Some foods just smell horrible! From hard boiled eggs to sardines, sometimes you need to redirect your nose from smelling what's going into your mouth. Comfortably slide fantastic device into your nostrils for a fresh breath of air up and away from that stinky food! Now if only Aunt Geraldine would stop serving her "signature" fish stew.

101 Unnecessary Inventions™ Congratulations, you are now a proud owner of one of my Unnecessary Inventions. Months of hard work in our laboratory creating my inventions has all led to this moment. You should really stop buying such unnecessary things.

USE THESE PAGES TO BRAINSTORM YOUR OWN INVENTION IDEAS!

Think you have what it takes to come up with your own Unnecessary Invention?

Send us your ideas at
www.unncessaryinventions.com
for a chance to see it brought to life!

Want to send us a note? Email us anytime at
hi@unnecessaryinventions.com

Be sure to follow us on Instagram, Facebook, and YouTube at @unnecessaryinventions.

Share your favorite invention on social media
with the hashtag:
#101UnnecessaryInventions